CURRICULUN

Curriculum Vitae

Lawrence Joseph

University of Pittsburgh Press

Published by the University of Pittsburgh Press, Pittsburgh, PA 15260

Feffer and Simons, Inc., London
Manufactured in the United States of America

Library of Congress Cataloging in Publication Data

Joseph, Lawrence.
Curriculum vitae.

(Pitt poetry series)
I. Title. II. Series.
PS3560.0775C87 1988 811'.54 87-27199
ISBN 0-8229-3577-5
ISBN 0-8229-5401-X (pbk.)

The author would like to thank the editors of the publications in which these poems, often in earlier versions, first appeared: *Boulevard* ("By the Way"); *Epoch* ("The Great Society"); *Michigan Quarterly Review* ("In the Beginning Was Lebanon" and "Sand Nigger"); *Ontario Review* ("Factory Rat," "My Grandma Weighed Almost Nothing," and "Rubaiyat"); *Partisan Review* ("I've Already Said More Than I Should"); *Pequod* ("In This Time," "Let Us Pray," and "Stop Me If I've Told You"); *Poetry* ("An Awful Lot Was Happening," "Any and All," "Curriculum Vitae," and "I Pay the Price"); *Poetry East* ("My Eyes Are Black as Hers," "There I Am Again," "This Much Was Mine," "This Is How It Happens," and "Who to Deny"); *Round & Catch* ("Mama Remembers"); *Stand* ("December 3, 1937"); and *Witness* ("In the Age of Post-capitalism").

"London" first appeared in the special one hundredth issue of *The Paris Review*.

"On Nature" first appeared in the seventy-fifth anniversary issue of *Poetry*.

"That's All," with a statement of its form, is included in *Ecstatic Occasions, Expedient Forms: Sixty-Five Leading Contemporary Poets Select and Comment on Their Poems* (New York: Macmillan, 1987).

"Any and All" also appears in the *Annual Survey of American Poetry, 1985* (New York: Roth, 1986).

The author also expresses gratitude to the National Endowment for the Arts for a 1984 poetry award.

The publication of this book is supported by grants from the National Endowment for the Arts in Washington, D.C., a Federal agency, and the Pennsylvania Council on the Arts.

For Nancy Van Goethem

Contents

Both in nature and in metaphor identity is
the vanishing-point of resemblance.

—Wallace Stevens

CURRICULUM VITAE

In the Age of Postcapitalism

The disabled garment worker
who explains to his daughter
he's God the Holy Spirit
and lonely and doesn't care
if he lives or dies;
the secret sarcoma shaped like a flower
in the bowels of a pregnant woman;
ashes in the river, a floating chair,
long, white, shrieking cats;
the watch that tells Zurich,
Jerusalem and Peking time;
and the commodities broker
nervously smiling, mouth slightly twitching
when he says to the police he's forgotten
where he left his Mercedes:
everything attaches itself to me today.
Thirty million—the American
Broadcasting Corporation World News
conservatively estimates—
murders already this century.
Whether the public debt
may have affected case history
Number 51's excuse that she was abandoned
on the pier by a dolphin
and the question "What Has Become of
the Question of 'I' "
are topics for discussion
at the Institute for Political Economy.
I know all about the transmigration of souls.
I know about love and about strife.
To delight in a measured phrase,
to bank the rage in the gut,
to speak more softly,
to waken at three in the morning to think only of her
—in the age of postcapitalism.

Yellow and gray dusk thickens around the Bridge.
Rain begins to slant between
the chimneys and the power plant.
I don't feel like changing,
or waiting anymore either,
and I don't believe we're dreaming
this October sixth, in New York City,
during the nineteen eighties.

My Eyes Are Black as Hers

Much did he see. Slowly
did he learn. Could not
realize himself significant
in a house of such magnitudes.

Mama held his tender awe.
She alone knew to touch,
sang to herself thoughts
of her own though never

did anyone listen but he.
He knew in her dresser
her powders and perfumes,
rose-colored creams.

He knew in her closets
stilled perfume of her dresses,
furs and silks and stockings,
the satin in the long cedar chest.

It was terribly hot—heatwave;
his patron saint's feast.
He said his prayers.
He said nine prayers:

Grandma and Grandma and Aunt Lila,
Aunt Adele, Mama, Aunt Ida,
and Aunt Jeanette—and God the Son,
and Mrs. Makdessi who has no one.

"This is a smart one," Mama says.
My eyes are black as hers.
"Too smart, I'm afraid—he'll
keep unhappy because of it,"

Mama said. I heard her.
That's what Mama said.
On the feast of my patron saint
that's what my Mama said.

Curriculum Vitae

I might have been born in Beirut,
not Detroit, with my right name.
Grandpa taught me to love to eat.
I am not Orthodox, or Sunni,
Shiite, or Druse. Baptized
in the one true Church, I too
was weaned on Saint Augustine.
Eisenhower never dreamed I wore
corrective shoes. Ford Motor Co.
never cared I'd never forgive
Highland Park, River Rouge, Hamtramck.
I memorized the Baltimore Catechism.
I collected holy cards, prayed
to a litany of saints to intercede
on behalf of my father who slept
through the sermon at 7 o'clock Mass.
He worked two jobs, believed
himself a failure. My brother
believed himself, my sister denied.
In the fifth grade Sister Victorine,
astonished, listened to me recite
from the Book of Jeremiah.
My voice changed. I wanted women.
The Jesuit whose yellow fingers
cracked with the stink of Camels
promised me eternal punishment.
How strange I was, with impure thoughts,
brown skin, obsessions.
You could tell by the way I walked
I possessed a lot of soul,
you could tell by the way I talked
I didn't know when to stop.
After I witnessed stabbings
outside the gym, after the game,

I witnessed fire in the streets.
My head set on fire in Cambridge,
England, in the Whim Café.
After I applied Substance and Procedure
and Statements of Facts
my head was heavy, was earth.
Now years have passed since I came
to the city of great fame.
The same sun glows gray on two new rivers.
Tears I want do not come.
I remain many different people
whose families populate half Detroit;
I hate the racket of the machines,
the oven's heat, curse
bossmen behind their backs.
I hear the inmates' collective murmur
in the jail on Beaubien Street.
I hear myself say, "What explains
the Bank of Lebanon's liquidity?"
think, "I too will declare
a doctrine upon whom the loss
of language must fall regardless
whether Wallace Stevens
understood senior indebtedness
in Greenwich Village in 1906."
One woman hears me in my sleep
plead the confusions of my dream.
I frequent the Café Dante, earn
my memories, repay my moods.
I am as good as my heart.
I am as good as the unemployed
who wait in long lines for money.

This Is How It Happens

This is how it happens, Paine
—says he's related in some way to Tom—

says, touching the moisture
on the side of his whiskey and ice.

The dollar declines, decreased
foreign investment. Consequently,

the deficit must be paid for
solely by Americans, crunching

the financial markets into inflation.
Interest rates exploding

while taxes rise! Expansion
never before so debt-ridden!

Expectations never so supreme.
Never have the happy been so well liked . . .

The day after Orpheus dies—
shot point-blank with a shotgun

by his father who, later questioned
whether he loved his son,

testified he couldn't say he disliked him—
the announcement of the latest fashion:

mink coats for men (Orpheus wore a tuxedo
at his press conference in Amsterdam

when, without hesitation,
he replied that his mission was to tell

about the upcoming holocaust
to whoever possessed the consciousness

to believe). And what about
that afternoon that August? Do you remember?

You worked in one room, through book
after book; two rooms away

she stretched a new canvas, the southern
light hot and almost red across her face

—who more alone, or afraid?
whose desires or volitions

less inexorable to each other's?
And what about your first brush

with fame? Serving Mass
for Father Coughlin in his Shrine

years after he'd been silenced by the Pope
—Coughlin! eloquently

ranting on the nature of money,
the mercy of Christ Militant,

the Christian Corporate State,
the Satan of the Jewish question

not in the central bank of Berlin;
no one cared what you thought about him,

no one cares now. Do you see?
Your mother, silent, her life

a series of disappointments.
Do you remember the first time

you saw a man your own age collapse
on the street from hunger and weakness?

Let's just say now it was
intentional when your hand brushed

against her blouse—the subtle knowledge of
who touches whom with which meanings.

Let's say the darkening of your voice
combined with an ever-increasing

refined sense of phrasing creates
religious intensity. And who could change

your purpose? Speaking a different tongue
in the Park where the two rivers

merge, or else by the oak benches
in some Court of Equity, your gaze

almost balanced. From the Heights,
through the Bridge's rows of iron

woven and girded in a silhouetted loom,
a woman might be seen closing her eyes

to think, or perhaps, later, to cry;
a woman, exhausted and sorrowful, might know

she must put on her face and forget
what just went through her mind.

Factory Rat

Hands of the West Virginian who insists
you're a Greek hillbilly and hands of Jesse
who insists "Can't be all that bad
if you a son of David"; long, bone-fingered
hands of Milton who wears his 57th
Infantry combat fatigues and your hands
at General Motors Truck & Coach in 1967
sandpaper primered bodies.
Imitate Milton: cut the thumb
and forefinger from a glove.
Squirt the foreman's eyes bleed;
he's drunk—"Don't sand with that
half-assed glove on"—the same night
the psycho pushing bodies onto the line
doesn't look and catches your knees. Jones,
at break time, excited about the girl
younger than his daughter he meets
on Sunday in a bar on Wide Track Road.
Pee Wee, nearby, negotiates with Red,
suddenly opens his mouth, wiggles
his tongue "They love it!"
The newspaper admits in July Pontiac burns
—do you want any trouble?
Forget the dust from the sandpapered primer
is flakes of metal. When Jesse
repeats "Hebrew!" and repeats
"What's the matter, Rabbi?" just smile.
When the relief man cheats cheat him back.
When you walk through the gate
you know the time. When a stranger asks
"Why's someone young as you work here?"
don't answer. You don't answer
when he answers "You're a factory rat like me."

I've Already Said More Than I Should

All that I know is that I know
my age from a face that was young

when I was, and is young no longer,
and the smell of salt from the East River

streaked black by black broken clouds
isn't mine to choose. When,

in the Hall of Oceanic Life, the waiter
brings medallions of veal, morels

and wild rice pilaf from a serving plate
onto my plate, 410 glasses

await 1979 Chateau Chasse-Spleen,
and in the past my grandma

walks with two oak canes
beneath the street's great silver maples

to the house I lived in my first year.
When, in this morning's paper,

the renowned poet and critic
professor is quoted decrying

the demise of English forms,
I write Esquire after my name.

This isn't an apology. I read
Fadi is too young to read, but

the message seems to have gotten through:
he vows he will kill who killed

his father and crush the bones.
This isn't a credo or a confession.

I make favors, complain, wear
a white shirt and blue suit. I'm tired.

I see controversy continues whether
the current situation is civil

commotion or war. "Fifty thousand
to 100,000 killed, a wracked

government, an army in barracks,
howitzers, tanks!" the president

of the insurance association's
property division lashes out in reply.

It isn't for nothing that I deny
interior theological dialogue, doubt

the existence of the new aeon,
don't sleep past dawn anymore.

In the offices of the great firm
whose name might matter

I won't reveal what I abhor,
or my desire, if I can't be rich,

to be, instead, moral or famous.
In the Desbrosses Street café

I order my third cappuccino al cognac,
light another cigarette,

confide to whoever listens
I've already said more than I should.

This Much Was Mine

Saturday morning, the June sun
already hot and white.
On the first tee,
Detroit Golf and Country Club,
the players, the caddies.
I am appointed Don Delaney's bag.
First, the bets:
one hundred dollars a nassau
five ways, automatic presses,
each player against the others.
Then, long drives lost
in the light and found
on the fairways, explosions
of grassblade and sand,
the quick roll and curve of the ball
from the apron onto the green.
On the eighteenth Delaney
asks how much club. I tell him,
he hits the seven iron
perfectly, one putts,
wins a lot of money.
You've probably forgotten
the stories in the national newsmagazines
years ago about "Dice" Delaney.
"Dapper of dress, genial of manner,
loud of voice," he gained
his reputation at craps,
hustled golf, made
the largest independent book in America
before his luck ran out.
Although I saw wonder when I saw
how much could be won
with skill and with calculation,
I hated his nervous face, his eyes
without color that couldn't

be still, the broken laughter
he feigned as he counted
combinations of money in his head.
I stuffed the crisp ten dollar bill
he paid me into my pocket.
I knew where it came from.
I knew this much was mine.

By the Way

What I saw was impossible
together. Only months between
the factories, furnaces
with hissing bronze pipes, smoke
streamed across flat skies,
and a woman named Mimi di Nescemi who exits
in black silk trousers, delicate heels;
a man who says his name is Ra
wrapped in blankets in a cardboard box
on Gold Street. I tried to explain.

On February second nineteen-seventy
at eight minutes past four
my father in his grocery store
perceived how desperate the man was
—he'd kill. The bullet missed
the spinal cord, miraculously,
the doctor said. Everything
eventually would be all right.
The event went uncelebrated among hundreds
of felonies in that city that day.

At lunch at the Broad Street Club
I couldn't stop looking at
the woman at the table across from me.
Beige-colored suit, blouse
unbuttoned two buttons, I could tell
she was sensual and smart and that
her presence hadn't gone unnoticed
by two bankers whose conversation
on floating exchange rates and computers
I couldn't help but overhear.

I couldn't help but overhear
my thoughts and opinions.
My starting point? Not Plato.
What if poverty and anger
and the desire for thrills,
and tribal attitudes, exist
not only on the streets but innately
—inherent, if you will,
within the boundaries of the nation,
social and economic classes, our time?

On public television, on a program
on national affairs, Mr. Getty
distinctly recalls his director's
emphasis: at one hundred dollars a share
or higher, the museum was a seller
not a buyer. "Which is a rhyme,"
Mr. Getty explains. "Put me among
the circle of poets for that.
That's the lowest circle
in Dante's hell, by the way."

In the Third Circle of Alexandria's
Department of Irrigation Services,
special clerk Constantine Kavafis
aggravated his imagination, thought
too much about the poet Lamon's
popularity (the rave of all
literary Beirut) and interpreted
the Asian blood in his veins.
In another circle, poets punctuate
their remarks with tics and odd sneezes.

In some circles, poets whip themselves
under every conceivable influence into mania
to advertise. In another room
a beautiful woman toward whom men always
try to be personal; which secrets,
which consciousness, cause her aloofness?
In the lowest circle in hell the Republic
has been betrayed, by the way.
In the lowest circle, shadows
seize skulls with their teeth.

In This Time

I

When you don't understand yet
the city's lungs are gray,
the shacks on wooden pillars,
salt heaps, scrap and cinders
breathe blood. When you can't
even imagine Grand River on fire.

When Czechlewski pronounces
"love is the mysterious
labyrinth that emanates
from the Divine." Your father
vomits every morning to ease
his nerves. Latin syllables
are counted, quantified.
Low blanket of yellow sky
inwardly summons prayer.

When you don't understand yet
the look in your face is fear.

II

In the Jesuit School
the middle voice
of the optative mood,
cassocks, wooden
kneelers, pages
of cosines, syllogisms.
In the imagination
the blue cotton skirt
at Immaculata High School
lifted with both hands.

In the Memorial Building
after the dance "when

the music begins to play
automatically you're
on your way." At home
the father returns late,
green work clothes
smeared with flesh
of animals he butchers.

III

It is blessed on Brush Street
beside the machine shop's junkyard
where hands are warmed
over fire in oil cans.
It is awesome, the poplar's shivering gold.
He is imitated, the soldier saint
who instructs that conversation,
if disordered, is sin.
She is praised whose tongue
opens your mouth in the damp basement.

It is enough sun behind blue smoke
to rent the elm buds, to burn the cloud's bloom.

IV

In this time a boy works
his mind beyond half dreams,
beyond the older woman alone
at midnight leaning toward him
from a windowsill, a thousand
chimneys hissing, the sudden
sweat from the April heat
broken down his backbone.

Already his heart
accepts its ceaseless weight.

Stop Me If I've Told You

That year, too, was finished.
Yellow fog vanished

in the lane of spring mistletoe,
Byron's Pool, Newton's rooms.

Emphatically, emphatically she said no
the second from the last time.

Her hair was light, bright red and beautiful.
She cried, I said don't.

While, drugged, I increased
to a very high power,

several billion dollars of bombs
dropped on Cambodia. Jerolds,

on Jesus Green, declared
he intended to be great.

R. A. H. Prince, at High Table,
observed Lewis' subtle depiction

of Eliot's eyes in the famous portrait
that hung in Hall, insisted

every American owned a car.
Stop me if I've told you about

the treatise on evil in the University Library,
purple rhododendrons

burst apart in midnight sun,
Paris, Thonon-les-Bains, Geneva in April,

my sensitivity, and my luck.
Home in November after my second Michaelmas

to find—myself. Myself
an abstraction; myself

drives to see the great factories,
wills his desire not to accumulate

in the brain, remembers
the Angelus' cadences

on the Shrine of the Little Flower's chimes.
Have I told you about

the Pillar of Families and the Hope
of the Sick, instants

of awareness, my own words
I should not comprehend?

July, in the village Ajaltoun
in the mountain in Lebanon

on the feast of Saint Elias,
while Beirut's heavy moon

and tin and cardboard houses
revolved behind my eyes,

I danced one step forward
and, then, one step to the side,

knelt, rose straightbacked,
upright in the beginnings

of some strange knowledge
I thought was true.

I vowed discipline. I vowed love.
I read all the books, believed

my irony my nostalgia reversed—
I believed it. January

in Cambridge, a new year,
I waken at dawn to walk

to the old Gasworks outside the city
toward familiar smells.

Mama Remembers

I tried to do what I was told, made
the sign of the cross before icons
of the Apostles and my prayer equal
fat Father Riashi sweating, incanting

Syriac surrounded by incense smoke
in Our Lady of Redemption Melchite Church
my fifth Palm Sunday. Did I know
arteries hardened, the business

was changed by years of no money,
there was a miscarriage, in January,
on Thursday, in the kitchen, in 1951?
Grandpa, legless, appeared to me alone

in dazzling hot September afternoon.
Mama could not know how not to be sad.
In the sunroom before the picture window
Aunt Rose and Aunt Angele compared

the color of my skin to old Uncle Moise's.
There was enough silence to divide.
My brother did not tell what he knew,
took his share, whatever he could.

Did I believe grandma's eyes revealed
her will to live or her need to die?
Mama remembers if my father ever cried.
Mama remembers how much she cried.

Sand Nigger

In the house in Detroit
in a room of shadows
when grandma reads her Arabic newspaper
it is difficult for me to follow her
word by word from right to left
and I do not understand
why she smiles about the Jews
who won't do business in Beirut
"because the Lebanese
are more Jew than Jew,"
or whether to believe her
that if I pray
to the holy card of Our Lady of Lebanon
I will share the miracle.
Lebanon is everywhere
in the house: in the kitchen
of steaming pots, leg of lamb
in the oven, plates of kousa,
hushwee rolled in cabbage,
dishes of olives, tomatoes, onions,
roasted chicken, and sweets;
at the card table in the sunroom
where grandpa teaches me
to wish the dice across the backgammon board
to the number I want;
Lebanon of mountains and sea,
of pine and almond trees,
of cedars in the service
of Solomon, Lebanon
of Babylonians, Phoenicians, Arabs, Turks
and Byzantines, of the one-eyed
monk, Saint Maron,
in whose rite I am baptized;
Lebanon of my mother
warning my father not to let

the children hear,
of my brother who hears
and from whose silence
I know there is something
I will never know; Lebanon
of grandpa giving me my first coin
secretly, secretly
holding my face in his hands,
kissing me and promising me
the whole world.
My father's vocal cords bleed;
he shouts too much
at his brother, his partner,
in the grocery store that fails.
I hide money in my drawer, I have
the talent to make myself heard.
I am admonished to learn,
never to dirty my hands
with sawdust and meat.
At dinner, a cousin
describes his niece's head
severed with bullets, in Beirut,
in civil war. "More than
an eye for an eye," he demands,
breaks down, and cries.
My uncle tells me to recognize
my duty, to use my mind,
to bargain, to succeed.
He turns the diamond ring
on his finger, asks if
I know what asbestosis is,
"the lungs become like this,"
he says, holding up a fist;
he is proud to practice
law which "distributes

money to compensate flesh."
Outside the house my practice
is not to respond to remarks
about my nose or the color of my skin.
"Sand nigger," I'm called,
and the name fits: I am
the light-skinned nigger
with black eyes and the look
difficult to figure—a look
of indifference, a look to kill—
a Levantine nigger
in the city on the strait
between the great lakes Erie and St. Clair
which has a reputation
for violence, an enthusiastically
bad-tempered sand nigger
who waves his hands, nice enough
to pass, Lebanese enough
to be against his brother,
with his brother against his cousin,
with cousin and brother
against the stranger.

Rubaiyat

All the stories about killing, burned bones, the smoke
from burning bones, a body tied by a rope fastened to a Mercedes
flying above the ground, cut-up body in a nylon bag,
black hoods, hallucinations, stylized hair and pure gold chains,

a report, according to the government official, forty-two
forced into the church and hacked to death with axes on the altar,
accounts confirmed by government officials a five-year-old boy
discovered nailed to a doorway in the form of a cross.

And what do you think you're doing when you want the names
and the years of the history, who begot whom and who made
which flesh which words that hate for which particular reasons
that compel the pride of the horrors of the oppressed?

That's how the brain talks, evil in its wakefulness.
It's just too crazy and it's too much and not unreal.
Fourteen years it's been now since Beirut's dust and the Shouf's sun
repressed. The crippled child without eyelashes spoke.

His face blue, his words didn't leave his mouth—
this is twelve years before Corporal McMahon in the bunker
"The Psycho Ward" beside the airport below Souk-al-Gharb
pokes at his C-rations, answers back home he liked to hunt geese.

Uncle Shikory three times a week took a bus to Beirut.
He did some deals in the back of some store. Talked slowly
in French about how little he remembered his brother, my
grandfather.
Angele, his daughter, frail and small, her husband dead ten years

—a cerebral hemorrhage. She wears layers of black.
He was only thirty-five and she isn't young. I hear her
weeping in the dark. Her eyes deep dark, sad and heavy.
She likes me—my moods. Once she touched my shoulders,

whispered, *d'accord, d'accord*. I've never forgotten that.
When I try consciously not to forget I surely will exhaust
the imagination. April. A year ago. In the Consul's residence.
Yasine Aballah Bacha. He asks if I know his family.

He too studied law—he and one of his bodyguards, Yousef Farsane.
Chartoun? He showed me an official map. Here it is
where the road from Damascus turns before Aleih. Captured
for obvious strategic reasons. At least twelve massacred,

one hundred forty-seven houses and the church destroyed.
I insult him if I don't smoke the Marlboro he offers,
don't drink Scotch whiskey first, before I drink coffee.
He calls the servant, a tall girl from Mauritania.

She became his when he was the Ambassador there, he says.
Lebanon is like Kafka, he says—emphasizing Kafka.
I should get in touch with him when I come to Los Angeles again;
he would like to introduce me to some of his friends.

You say the Shah of Baabda sits like a crow on the head
of the gangster from Syria who kisses both ears of the Sheik
of Zaghorta who secretly covets the Prince of Moukharta's access
through State Department intermediaries to the King of Israel—

who cares that your politics change, that you change,
that a sharp nausea plugs your chest, blood quickened
with the harmonies of numbers counted, realized, and forgotten?
It is no time to be uncertain about what has happened or what can.

What has Angele seen? What has she had to put into her brain?
Uncle Shikory's insane; the nuns in the mountain take care of him.
Where is Angele? Gone with the others into the mountain?
Where is Angele? Her eyes were heavy. She wore black ten years.

In the Beginning Was Lebanon

In the beginning was Lebanon,
a mountain of musk and the sea
above a star, and the star, Son
of Ali, massacred on a hill
of Galilee grown smooth from rain,
and the rain, oil that washed
skulls and jawbones and pelvises
of children back into red sand
was with God; and the Lebanon
was God. God of high, polished
black boots, faces masked
with black hoods, compounded
of two elements and a single will
to seek vengeance from Abbasids,
Druse, Palestinians, who sits
at the right hand of a swimming
pool in the villa of Saint George
in the kingdom of the Knights
Templar, God who assumes the body
of the father in the holy tomb,
blue-haired or gray-eyed
God who transforms Moslems into dogs
with painted coats, Christians
into slaves with discs in their ears,
God who denies any heart lifted
toward the screen of giant clover,
ignorant God of the great wars
and the families who, reincarnated,
is English and who, beneath
a photograph of Father Abraham,
dozes before bread and sweet milk
above Massar-es-Shouf, this God
who changes tears into bombs
of phosphorous in the eyes of the dumb,

God of the villages named after blood
who, like the sea, sees the houses
at its bottom, who, like the star,
pours down its promises on the Feasts
of the Pigs, who, like fire,
burns the sea and our stomachs
and the brain of the child
who stumbles against the earth around which
brothers and sisters wail.

That's All

I work and I remember. I conceive
a river of cracked hands above Manhattan.

No spirit leaped with me in the womb.
No prophet explains why Korean women

thread Atomic Machinery's machines
behind massive, empty criminal tombs.

Why do I make my fire my heart's blood,
two or three ideas thought through

to their conclusions, make my air
dirty the rain around towers of iron,

a brown moon, the whole world?
My power becomes my sorrow.

Truth? My lies are sometimes true.
Firsthand, I now see the God

whose witness is revealed in tongues
before the Exchange on Broad Street

and the transfer of 2,675,000,000 dollars
by tender offer are acts of the mind,

and the calculated truths of First
National City Bank. Too often

I think about third cousins in the Shouf.
I also often think about the fact that

in 1926, after Céline visited
the Ford Rouge foundry and wrote

his treatise on the use of physically
inferior production line workers,

an officially categorized "displaced person"
tied a handkerchief around his face

to breathe the smells and the heat
in a manner so as not to destroy

his lungs and brain for four years
until he was laid off. I don't

meditate on hope and despair.
I don't deny the court that rules

my race is Jewish or Abyssinian.
In good times I transform myself

into the sun's great weight, in bad times
I make myself like smoke on flat wastes.

I don't know why I choose who I am:
I work and I remember, that's all.

Who to Deny

I see him before dawn, roused
from sleep by the clatter
of a train over a distant viaduct
and the horns of a freighter
ringing in his ears. I see him
at his job, working volumes
of testimony, fleshing facts.
At the Capitol he argues strategy
to use in opinions
he writes for the Chief Justice,
at lunch at the Grecian Gardens
with Levin—broiled chicken,
fried potatoes, salad—
he agrees: Jimmy Hoffa's body
was sizzled in some warehouse
incinerator in Hamtramck.
Who to deny he knows
annals of businesses out of existence
and his history?—he knows
the number of crimes since 1963.
When she moves her leg to let
her dress above her knee
she catches his eye. Who to deny
he's right there, in the heart of it:
on the bus preoccupied
with his books. Doctor Stavros
prescribes medication
for his pain. Ten years and a war
it takes to learn to ask the price of things
before touching them.
I see him at Grace Hospital.
His father-in-law is dying.
He looks at him, starts to cry—
he cannot attempt to describe.
He helps count what's left behind:

shirts, shoes, documents.
I see him at Saint Anne's. Consciously
taking light from the stained glass,
unashamed to pray—
no act of hope or faith, but to ease
all he doesn't know how to shake.
Later, at the café on Agnes Street,
cup after cup of coffee. Later,
the wind reddens and burns his face.
Later you find him in Grand Circus Park.
The manifesto stuck to the statue
of Mayor Hazen Pingree
of a worker reaching for the sky
against a factory background.
An obscure essay on beauty by Simone Weil
tests him. If you really must know,
he isn't unhappy.

December 3, 1937

Not in Budapest beside the powerful dark Danube,
but at a railroad station in a village on Lake Balaton.

A shivering idiot, the moon and the stars witnessed.
Why, when you lay your arm across the track

did you kneel, poet? Cumanian, half Szeklar, half Rumanian
that right arm later found cleanly severed

a hundred feet away from your body mangled
under the wheels of the howling train carrying your freight:

pig snouts and iron and ulcers and greasy dusks
and legs trembling from too much weight.

Why did your women find in your bedroom drawer
a shirt from which you cut off the right sleeve?

Did you believe you would only lose the choice
to pick up a pen again and write? József,

the idiot drooled and giggled when he told how you died,
how your heart burst through your large black eyes.

An Awful Lot Was Happening

When you come down to particulars everything's more complicated.
Fervent gestures in the South U restaurant, even the Greeks
behind the counter listen. Burned draft cards,
lamb's blood poured over files at the downtown draft board
—acts of resistance, moral values begun.

Saint Augustine in *De Trinitate* didn't see memory structured
by public events. A great moment in my life—not purple clouds
which excited my longings in Nichols Arboretum;
instead, the rumor cancer spread through Lyndon Johnson's brain.
Saint Augustine in his *Enchiridion ad Laurentium* didn't see

her dress and bra across the only chair in my small room
at One Thousand Four Olivia. I couldn't comprehend
whether more words might mean more, my greed, untrained,
not yet certain of its justifications.
And there was war. And from the bluffs above the Huron River

rain of starlight above Ann Arbor's lights, three, four
bell chimes ringing in the Tower. It wasn't Rome.
She dizzied me with excessive desires and thoughts.
What I wanted from all my talk of beauty, she said, was power,
and because of it, she said, I'd cause much suffering.

Although I never bragged misery—maybe once. I was serious.
What was I supposed to do when I heard you could be beaten or worse
in the neighborhood in Detroit between Linwood and Dexter,
the color of your eyes wrong. These are facts.
Professor Fuller's response that no one taught them to be quiet.

Glass from the bank's large plated windows all over the street.
I telephoned—line busy; tried again a few minutes later
—no answer. Where is she?—the verge of tears.
Swinburnian dactyls merely went through my ears. Advocated
concision, spatial range, temporal disposition of simple language.

And didn't the spokesman for the Black Action Movement
also receive a number over three hundred in the draft lottery
and attend graduate school? —I came back.
Three years later, every space turned inside out.
January, noon, beams of light across you shake out. Confused,

whirling joy when you slid off me. I leaned
again to embrace you. Uniform Commercial Code on the table.
On the dresser, a cup of coffee, tulips in a vase.
How to explain to myself how much I love you.
In the Law Quadrangle—my peer. He commanded Marines

in the Anhoa Basin. What did I know—what hookworms are like.
What it's like to shoot a Viet Cong, popped from a hole, in the eye.
A piece of metal in your kidney. It's too easy
to be sheep, he concludes, softly. Or too difficult,
I add, softly. He stares at me and whispers something.

When I answered I intended to maintain freedom my brother was
 riled.
What, or who, collides in you beside whose body I sleep?
No work at Tool & Die, Motors, Transmission, or Tractor
while the price of American crude rises another dollar.
There really wasn't enough work anywhere. And there was war

God the spirit of holy tongues couldn't release me from,
or from my dumbness. Pressured—delirious—
from too much inductive thinking, I waited for
the image in whose presence the heart opens and opens
and lived to sleep well; of necessity assessed earth's profit

in green and red May twilight. —You came toward me
in your black skirt, white blouse rolled at the sleeves.
Anticipation of your eyes, your loose hair!
My elementary needs—to cohere, to control.
An awful lot was happening and I wanted more.

I Pay the Price

Memory slipping more and more,
whole days no longer exist.

It's not that I don't feel well.
Pulse 77, 76, I've learned

nothing will pass. Yesterday
the news full of dead,

the Dictionary on Historical Principles
open on the table

at the definition of sentiment,
today I hear market analysts

expectantly attend the latest
conferences on chaos.

Before the picture window vista
of the East River, I hear Miss

Newman—she insists she be called
Miss—expound her aesthetic.

"This city, the ultimate art!
Masses of steel and light

jutted beyond heaven, a miracle
that is human and works."

This city of my own, dull gray,
rose, yellow, murky pink skies.

I know what I'm saying. I know
tomorrow I may forget

the man whom I see tonight
on Pearl Street under the Bridge

who appears at first to have no head.
He asks me to tell him

who he is, to take him, please,
to the police. He is sick,

mentally. He hasn't controlled
his bladder or his bowels.

Tomorrow I've also a big day ahead of me
protecting interests.

Though I don't have the appropriate letters
to get where I want,

my progress continues.
I distance myself to see myself

say to myself even before
I hang up the telephone, "I love this!"

From my apartment, from which I've a good view
of the same Bridge, I watch

a workman standing on the pier, looking
across at the coast turning toward

the Narrows, his hands bandaged,
victim of a work accident

who doesn't know what to think
or what to do and hasn't enough

to buy himself something to settle his mind.
I walk about my rooms

composing arguments in my defense.
"Live and die before a mirror,"

Baudelaire says, sipping espresso
at the corner of Hudson and Barrow.

I live in words and off my flesh
in order to pay the price.

When the ancient fury persists,
I pay the price.

Let Us Pray

My name is Lawrence Joseph,
in the name of my father
Joseph, who's also my son,
and in the name of the women

who receive me. I confess
too much. For my penance:
corporal works of mercy.
Who cleansed the prophet Isaias

with a burning coal deign
purify me that I may worthily
proclaim. Let me pray.
At the time the greatest

commandment was to seize
the light, I was light;
in those days innocence
rescued. Let us pray.

We cry from what makes sense.
Our flesh, resurrected,
multiplies and divides
into countless fiery tongues.

Let your cry come to me.
I will not forsake you,
I, Lawrence Joseph, loved so much
by your pain and your beauty.

The Great Society

Where my mother prayed for my birth
no more confessionals or votive candles
or statue of Blessed Martin de Porres.
A flock of swans above Belle Isle.
Grease in the river and in my hair.

A Great Society, the President declares
in the football stadium eleven miles
from the sign "Welcome to Romulus
Where Healthy Plants Grow." Why
shouldn't my father cheat the wholesaler

to sell to the poor at less loss
or my cousin sing, "Can't forget
the Motor City." On a clear day
the Mayor replaces houses with weeds,
sees the White House. *Bands of roving*

Negro youths, tonight, on Joseph Campau . . .
Szabo crushes beer cans on his skull.
Unskilled labor's wanted at Eldon Axle.
He who soon will need to kill Vietnamese
memorizes Malcolm. After the crowd

outside the blind pig does not disperse
it is difficult to explain to someone
who is not there the 101st Airborne
at the State Fairgrounds, fifty caliber
machine guns mounted on tanks, bazookas.

Brush Street at midnight, the child
huddled with a toy, eerie silence.
Wind brings balm in April, in August
hours of lightning but no rain.
The power of place, the power to demand

an answer from myself, the factories,
the girl whose breasts make me wild,
the communion of saints, streets.
Earth pouring clouds into gray heavens.
Much more violence than I know.

London

Aged malt whiskey and cigarettes
    consumed to enhance consciousness
—read Blake. You can't regulate
    the price of necessaries
without destruction. In a bar
    a few streets from the British Museum
across the table from Oxford's
    latest rising literary star;
not much older than you, his
    history is already impressive.
"There are rules, aren't there,"
    he shrugs, agitatedly,
"and decorum, and irony,"
    he clears his throat and, then,
vanishes behind the Royal Exchange,
    beyond the intent stare
of someone, somewhere, aggrieved
    and the student from the Polytechnic
who laughs after he announces
    he's schizophrenic before he, too,
vanishes down a small lane
    behind the old synagogue
away from where you walk alone
    along Victoria Embankment.
—The sky was low, always low,
    often clear, or raw. You were
the "you" aware of the spite
    and the sorrow. Spirit
to the bone set loose, sensed,
    certain violence. Spirit
in the blood set loose, moved
    by cold smoke from the rows
evaporating. Those whose faces
    thrust forward, gaunt, no chins,

no more eyes—that kind of look
    possessed. It happened;
it wasn't misunderstanding when that woman
    said she never could have
had or have what you have,
    looked away, too sensitive.
An argument on the last train
    from Cambridge to King's Cross
about—the extent of His
    Lordship's estate. The poplar's shadow,
darker than the bluish light,
    spread across complete silence
on the Green at midnight.
    The fact, in Glasgow, straight
razors were means to threaten
    or deter; the fact we are victims
of our truths was true.
    You ought not to have been
what you were, what you
    might have been was a simple fate
in a bag of wind. Nothingness
    erupted. Everything foretold.

Any and All

You draw nearer to see her more closely,
the blind woman by the bronze doors

of the old Merchants Bank, her mouth
wide open as if in a silent roar,

several dollars stuffed in the pockets
of her mink coat. She is easy to forget

a few days later when you think of her
—not long. The phone is ringing.

You put Byrdman on hold. Polen
wants you in his office immediately.

The lawyers from Mars and the bankers
from Switzerland have arrived to close the deal,

the money in their heads articulated
to the debt of the state of Bolivia.

How much later the Croatian woman
who empties the wastebaskets laughs

when you answer you've been better
and you've been worse. How much sooner

you're told not to tell anyone Byrdman's
grandfather was a Jew. How much No. 54

Wall Street, emblematic reality of extreme
speculations and final effects.

The other evening at a party in the West Sixties
you say as much. None of them knows

what any of it is worth, you say to yourself
later, spitting into an unexpected breeze.

Yellow moons of street lamps on Ninth Avenue
obscured by atmospheric soot and fog,

in the Twenties empty windows of butcher shops,
factories and warehouses without names,

no taxis, the green light behind the window
of a corner bar. A young man sporting muscles,

a woman he might own on his arm, clearly
doesn't like the way you look or look at him,

lets his leash out enough for his wolfdog
to just nip your leg. Another day

you contemplate your strategy:
think about how they think about you

thinking about them and the look on your face
to prove you have the proper attitude.

Let no laughter reveal moods. Let
Charlotte Stone reveal that her father

over the weekend purchased a peninsula in Rhode Island
for Harry and her, let her teeth

be too large and too gray: there is blood
and there is blood-letting; this is not your blood.

Shut the door and wait. Someone else's father
forgives you when you know not what you do,

reminds you, "He's a weasel but he's my friend."
You're a monkey and you work for him,

decide for him whether his clauses should be restrictive,
whether to replace every "any" with "all."

My Grandma Weighed Almost Nothing

It was that April morning that the weight
of tumor mass eroded her frontal bone
through her dura to the brain's substance,

through the corridor of junipers on the road
to Aleih, before the blood of the Great War
dried, and the priest beat Tanous's head

in Hadeth? or was it Chartoun? her cousin
with his large brown, black eyes agreed
and she agreed, in that month of mists,

although Najla burned with whooping cough
and the sun, and mosquitoes ruined the olives,
in that hour of dark blue night, the year

1912 or 1913, wrapped in blankets while sea
turned over toward Marseilles and the island
Ellis became the beautiful valley and the lakes

Ontario and Erie, and the voice on the train
said, Detroit, and she said that word again,
Detroit, before the cold air behind the maples

on Livernois cracked yellow, before Alfred,
in his new suit, bragged Purple Gang
to Angele, in the store on Cass and Temple.

—She couldn't hold herself up, or sleep
and dream dreams she didn't want. She rubbed
her bald skull. My grandma weighed almost

nothing—arms folded around her like sea
and its algae, old sea softened into a Boulevard
or heat or sleep and silence ten times

pain that made her weight her bones
and one or two tears she cried alone
in Women's Hospital that April—then died.

On Nature

To proceed: whether results are evident
because they're results. Mists
from chromeplate parts precipitate
ulcers of the skin and cancer.
Raw, hard sun becoming stronger.
Should I save my pity for myself?
Do to others what's been done to you?
Unlimited desires at age thirty-seven
moved to tears before a rose.
It makes sense that the socialist regime
enters into a series of contracts
with private corporations to produce
and market its oil resources.
The data actually proves it's difficult
to draw conclusions on the fate
of the lower middle class. Will
the sophora tree maintain its distinctness?
Free potatoes, trucked from another state,
feeding those reconciled to their doom.
Pork fat? Ten to 24 million tons of dust,
loss of light north of the equator,
temperature drop of 18 to 55 degrees
depending on the season. August afternoon
velveted with drink, softened
yellow; floundering marsh, iron river,
blue, heavy air in the bloodstream.
Everyone has some, no one has enough,
but if you have the will you'll be taken care of.
When imported shoes mean the state
of the economy isn't prosperous?
Water with nothing but a little lemon in it.
The woman in bed turning toward
her husband drowsing in a chair?

You get nothing for nothing and a rat's
human as a cat, and the bird
with wild open wings creates a counterlight.
Cool metallic shimmering on the Avenue.
Your eyes I can't take mine from.
Will you love me more if I remain silent?
Even the belief in metamorphosis
after awhile doesn't bother me.

There I Am Again

I see it again, at dusk, half darkness in its brown light,
large tenements with pillars on Hendrie beside it,

the gas station and garage on John R beside it,
sounds of acappella from a window somewhere, pure, nearby it

pouring through the smell of fried pork to welcome
whoever enters it to do business.

Today, again, in the second year of the fifth recession
my father holds pickled feets, stomachs and hearts,

I lift crates of okra and cabbages,
let down crates of buttermilk and beer,

bring live carp to the scale and come, at last, to respect
the intelligence of roaches in barrels of bottles,

I sell the blood on the wooden floor after the robbery,
salt pork and mustard greens and Silver Satin wine,

but only if you pay, down, on the counter
money you swear you'll never hand over, only if,

for collateral, you don't forget you too may have to kill.
Today, again, in the third year of unlimited prosperity,

the Sunday night the city burns
I hear sirens, I hear broken glass, I believe

the shadow of my father's hand that touches my hair,
my cousin loading a carbine, my uncle losing his mind

today in a place the length of a pig's snout
in a time the depth of a cow's brain

in Joseph's Market on the corner of John R and Hendrie
there I am again: always, everywhere,

apron on, alone behind the cash register, the grocer's son
angry, ashamed, and proud as the poor with whom he deals.

About the Author

Lawrence Joseph was born in Detroit, Michigan, in 1948. His grandparents were Lebanese and Syrian Catholic immigrants. He was educated at the University of Michigan, where he won the Hopwood Award for Poetry; Magdalene College, Cambridge University, where he read English literature; and the University of Michigan Law School. His first book of poems, *Shouting at No One,* received the 1982 Agnes Lynch Starrett Poetry Prize, and was published in the Pitt Poetry Series in 1983. His poems have appeared in *The Paris Review, Poetry, Ontario Review, Partisan Review,* and other magazines. Among his awards is a 1984 National Endowment for the Arts Poetry Fellowship. A professor of law at St. John's University School of Law, he lives in New York City.

PITT POETRY SERIES

Ed Ochester, General Editor

Dannie Abse, *Collected Poems*
Claribel Alegría, *Flowers from the Volcano*
Jon Anderson, *Death and Friends*
Jon Anderson, *In Sepia*
Jon Anderson, *Looking for Jonathan*
Maggie Anderson, *Cold Comfort*
Michael Benedikt, *The Badminton at Great Barrington; Or, Gustave Mahler & the Chattanooga Choo-Choo*
Michael Burkard, *Ruby for Grief*
Kathy Callaway, *Heart of the Garfish*
Siv Cedering, *Letters from the Floating World*
Lorna Dee Cervantes, *Emplumada*
Robert Coles, *A Festering Sweetness: Poems of American People*
Kate Daniels, *The White Wave*
Norman Dubie, *Alehouse Sonnets*
Stuart Dybek, *Brass Knuckles*
Odysseus Elytis, *The Axion Esti*
Jane Flanders, *Timepiece*
Brendan Galvin, *The Minutes No One Owns*
Gary Gildner, *Blue Like the Heavens: New & Selected Poems*
Bruce Guernsey, *January Thaw*
Michael S. Harper, *Song: I Want a Witness*
Barbara Helfgott Hyett, *In Evidence: Poems of the Liberation of Nazi Concentration Camps*
Milne Holton and Paul Vangelisti, eds., *The New Polish Poetry: A Bilingual Collection*
David Huddle, *Paper Boy*
Phyllis Janowitz, *Temporary Dwellings*
Lawrence Joseph, *Curriculum Vitae*
Lawrence Joseph, *Shouting at No One*
Shirley Kaufman, *From One Life to Another*
Shirley Kaufman, *Gold Country*
Etheridge Knight, *The Essential Etheridge Knight*
Ted Kooser, *One World at a Time*
Ted Kooser, *Sure Signs: New and Selected Poems*
Larry Levis, *Winter Stars*
Larry Levis, *Wrecking Crew*
Robert Louthan, *Living in Code*
Tom Lowenstein, tr., *Eskimo Poems from Canada and Greenland*

Archibald MacLeish, *The Great American Fourth of July Parade*
Peter Meinke, *Night Watch on the Chesapeake*
Peter Meinke, *Trying to Surprise God*
Judith Minty, *In the Presence of Mothers*
Carol Muske, *Camouflage*
Carol Muske, *Wyndmere*
Leonard Nathan, *Carrying On: New & Selected Poems*
Leonard Nathan, *Holding Patterns*
Kathleen Norris, *The Middle of the World*
Sharon Olds, *Satan Says*
Alicia Ostriker, *The Imaginary Lover*
Greg Pape, *Black Branches*
Greg Pape, *Border Crossings*
James Reiss, *Express*
William Pitt Root, *Faultdancing*
Liz Rosenberg, *The Fire Music*
Herbert Scott, *Groceries*
Richard Shelton, *Selected Poems, 1969-1981*
Peggy Shumaker, *The Circle of Totems*
Arthur Smith, *Elegy on Independence Day*
Gary Soto, *Black Hair*
Gary Soto, *The Elements of San Joaquin*
Gary Soto, *The Tale of Sunlight*
Gary Soto, *Where Sparrows Work Hard*
Tomas Tranströmer, *Windows & Stones: Selected Poems*
Chase Twichell, *Northern Spy*
Chase Twichell, *The Odds*
Leslie Ullman, *Dreams by No One's Daughter*
Constance Urdang, *The Lone Woman and Others*
Constance Urdang, *Only the World*
Ronald Wallace, *People and Dog in the Sun*
Ronald Wallace, *Tunes for Bears to Dance To*
Cary Waterman, *The Salamander Migration and Other Poems*
Bruce Weigl, *A Romance*
Robley Wilson, Jr., *Kingdoms of the Ordinary*
David Wojahn, *Glassworks*
David P. Young, *The Names of a Hare in English*
Paul Zimmer, *Family Reunion: Selected and New Poems*